MW00780469

The
Dictionary
of
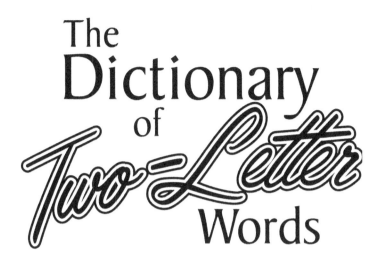
Words

THE SCRABBLE PLAYER'S
SECRET WEAPON!

Master the Building-Blocks of the Game with
Memorable Definitions of All 127 Words

RICK CARLILE

The Dictionary of Two-Letter Words — The Scrabble Player's Secret Weapon!
Master the Building-Blocks of the Game with Memorable Definitions of All 127 Words

By Rick Carlile

Copyright © 2019 Rick Carlile. All rights reserved. Except for use in a review, no part of this book may be reproduced or transmitted in any form or by any means, electronic or mechanical, including photocopying, recording, or otherwise, or by any information storage and/or retrieval system, without prior written permission from the publisher.

Cover design by Carlile Media
First edition published 2019 by Carlile Media
Published in the United States of America

ISBN-13: 978-1-949117-12-7
ISBN-10: 194911712X

"UOL Mind" books help create and sustain a healthy rational mind. They are part of the "University of Life Library," intended to bring the benefits of a university education to all.

WWW.CARLILE.MEDIA

A DIVISION OF CREADYNE DEVELOPMENTS LLC, LAS VEGAS, NV

TABLE OF CONTENTS

INTRODUCTION

Two-letter words are not only the basic building-blocks of Scrabble, they are the anchor-points upon which our most fantastic and high-scoring words depend. Creating words from our available tiles is only half the battle: fitting them into the existing words on the board is if anything the trickier part of the game.

Two-letter words are also our refuge when grander opportunities fail to appear, and can themselves provide extremely satisfying and elegant high scores — spotting a vacant triple-letter bonus atop an "A" when one holds a "ZA," or above an "I" when one holds a "QI" is an elating moment and a quick, graceful route to a terrific, foe-crushing move.

The competitive Scrabble player *must* therefore develop a knowledge of and facility with these elusive two-letter words. There is simply no other way to take full advantage of the opportunities of the game. When you possess such an easy familiarity, your opponents will wonder how you are able to dominate the board and place your words with such apparent ease!

After all, in Scrabble as in the rest of life, making it look easy is the ultimate skill.

MEMORIZATION

The major problem with memorizing Scrabble's two-letter words is that at first glance many of them appear unfamiliar and nonsensical. There is often also a somewhat opaque delineation between what is permissible and what is not, and so reason alone is an insufficient guide.

It is therefore vital for the equipped player not only to be aware of the permitted words' existence, but to *know* them. It should be fairly uncontroversial to suggest that words denote and connote concepts and therefore to "know" a word without being aware of its meaning is not to know it at all. A word-list alone would thus be suboptimal; definitions are key to creating a mental picture of the object or concept a word represents. When such a picture exists in the memory, the owner-operator of that memory can access one from the other — he/she has a three-dimensional grasp of the concept.

That said, we all remember things in somewhat different ways: for some, rote learning is effective; for others a visual image is primary (though the nature of that picture should originate from the individual for maximum impact and durability).

Therefore, this slim volume offers the following aides-mémoire to the reader:

- Explanatory definitions of every allowed two-letter word, including any interesting (in our opinion) background facts and/or memorable etymological notes.

- A mnemonic phrase after each definition, starting "Remember [...]" designed to encourage prompt recall by lodging the word in your memory, connected to a well-known saying, pun, or mental image. It is an odd quirk of human nature that a bad pun or clichéd phrase will stick in the memory (and the craw) more effectively than a good joke or elegant verbiage, and consequently no apology whatsoever is offered for the corniness or irritating nature of these phrases.

- Plural forms for all words, where applicable. In cases where the addition of an "s" creates an allowable word, even when the word is not (or not primarily) the plural form, it is also included — for example, "ha" and "has."

- Full reference word-lists arranged by starting and ending letters, which can assist memorization by repetition.

- Margin space for you to add your own phrases, drawings, etc.

- Pages for your own notes, etc. Also useful for writing in any new words to be added to the list in future.

THE OFFICIAL WORD LISTS

There are two official Scrabble word lists in operation, distinguished by the geographical areas in which they are used for tournament play. The *Official Tournament and Club Word List* (abbreviated "OTCWL," "OWL" or "TWL") was used in the United States of America, Canada and Thailand until its replacement by the *North American Scrabble Players' Association Word List* (*NASPA Word List* or *NWL)* in March of 2019, whereas the *Collins Scrabble Words* list (abbreviated "CSW" and also known as "SOWPODS," referring to an anagrammatic combination of the acronyms for the *Official Scrabble Players Dictionary* and *Official Scrabble Words* list[1]) is used in the rest of the English-speaking world.

The practical difference to permitted two-letter words is small, but important. At the time of writing, NWL contains one hundred and seven

---

1. Although "DO SWOPS" might have been a more apt anagram, "swop" being a (UK spelling) synonym for "exchange," as in to exchange tiles.

two-letter words[1], whereas CSW adds twenty[2] for a total of one hundred and twenty-seven words (all NWL two-letter words are also in CSW).

Therefore, this book includes separate NWL and CSW lists, as well as a list of the additional CSW words. Furthermore, the dictionary includes the following indicator for CSW-only words:

(i) **CSW ONLY**

When a CSW-only word's plural is also CSW-only, no additional indicator is added. However, when a CSW-only word's plural is also to be found in NWL, or an NWL word's plural is CSW-only, this information is included.

Pronunciation of Greek letters is provided consistent with their use in English science and mathematics (etc.), not modern Greek usage.

Good luck in your games!

---

1. Including recent additions "EW" and "OK."
2. Many sources claim nineteen additional words, but "ZE" was recently added.

A

AA

PL.: AAS

A type of lava. Found geologically in Hawaii, from whose language the word originates. Pronounced "ah-ah." Remember that "aa" is always found in "lAvA" (and also HAwAii).

AB

PL.: ABS

Abbr. of "abdominal" (muscles): remember not to neglect your ABs.

AD

PL.: ADS

Abbr. of "advertisement." Remember that ADs are everywhere, AD nauseam.

AE

PL.: N/A

Alternative version of "one" (largely Scots). Also a ligature appearing in Latin and Latin transliteration of Greek words. Remember this for AEons.

AG

PL.: AGS

Abbr. of "agriculture." Remember "Go AGgies!" (Texas Agricultural & Medical University football).

AH

PL.: AHS

Exclamation of surprise, pleasure, etc. Remember to be pleasantly surprised when you can use a 4-point "H": "AH!"

AI
PL.: AIS

A type of three-toed sloth native to Brazil, pronounced "ah-ee." Remember: though sloth is a sin, this one will AId you with its Artificial Intelligence.

AL
PL.: ALS

Tree found in East India, known as the "Indian mulberry," also a creature from Persian folklore said to interfere with childbirth. Remember, you can call me "AL."

AM
PL.: N/A

First person singular present of "to be." Remember this in the AM and all day long.

AN
PL.: N/A

Indefinite article used before words beginning with a vowel. Remember this and you have AN ANgle on a good score.

AR
PL.: ARS

Phonetic spelling of the letter "R." Remember why pirates are cool: because they just ARrrr.

AS
PL.: ASS

Comparative used to indicate similar degree or contemporaneity. Remember this AS long AS you can.

AT
PL.: N/A

Indicates the location or time of a thing or event. Remember that you forget this AT your peril.

PL.: N/A

Expression of various emotions including sympathy, disbelief, etc. Remember this to get an AWesome score.

Note that the plural "aws" is not currently an official Scrabble word.

AX

PL.: AXES

Variant of "axe." Remember not to AX stupid questions.

AY

PL.: AYS

Variant of "aye." Remember to vote AY.

B

BA
PL.: BAS

A spiritual entity in Egyptian mythology; part of the human soul along with the "ka" (see also). Remember this is not a BAd word.

BE
PL.: BES

To exist, occur or take place. Remember to BE good.

The "plural" "bes" is in fact an alternate term for "beth," the second letter of the Hebrew alphabet.

BI
PL.: BIS

Abbr. of "bisexual." Remember to BI groceries.

The plural "bis" also means "twice" or "again," used synonymously with "encore."

BO
PL.: BOS

Staff used in Japanese martial arts, friend (corruption of "beau") and a type of fig tree found in India. Remember to kiss your BO or he/she may hit you with a BO.

BY
PL.: BYS

Alongside, or to indicate the passing of something. Remember to BY groceries!

The plural "bys" mainly relates to the use of "by" to mean a "pass" in some card games.

C

CH

(i) **CSW ONLY**

PL.: N/A

An archaic version of the first person singular "I." Derives via Old English from the Proto-Germanic "ek" or "ik" root, which gives us the modern German "ich" and Dutch "ik." Remember: this word, meaning "ego" or "self," should strike a CHord in your CHaracter.

D

DA
PL.: DAS

Father. Remember this as the German affirmative: DA, ist gut.

DE
PL.: N/A

Latin- or French-derived preposition meaning "of" or "from" as in "de jure" or "coup de main." Remember, this move could be your coup DE grace.

DI

A syllable used when vocalizing a tune or rhythm.

(i) **CSW ONLY**

PL.: DIS (CSW & NWL)

Note that the plural "dis" is found in both CSW and NWL word lists under a rather stronger definition: to disrespect (also "diss").

DO
PL.: DOS

To perform an action. Also a note on the sol-fa diatonic scale (see "fa"). Remember to DO your best.

E

EA

 CSW ONLY

PL.: EAS

A river or other flowing water. Remember this word and you will grin from EA to EA.

ED

PL.: EDS

Abbr. of "education" (and its variants). Remember to use your 'ED for an EDifying move.

EE

 CSW ONLY

PL.: N/A

Archaic Scottish (and northern English) term for an eye. Also a northern English interjection expressing a wide variety of emotions. Remember to use your EEs to sEE when you can use this word.

Note that the plural "ees" is not currently an official Scrabble word.

EF

PL.: EFS

Phonetic spelling of the letter "F." Remember the inEFfable nature of the divine.

EH

PL.: EHS (CSW ONLY)

Exclamation expressing incomprehension or surprise. Remember to make EH while the sun shines.

EL

PL.: ELS

An elevated railroad, as in Chicago, also the phonetic rendering of the letter "L" and a deity in Canaanite folklore. Remember that if you forget this there will be EL to pay.

EM

PL.: EMS

Phonetic spelling of the letter "M" and a printer's term for a type of dash ("em dash"). EMphatically r-EM-EM-ber this one.

EN

PL.: ENS

Another printer's dash ("en dash") and phonetic spelling of the letter "N." Remember to ENliven a dull turn.

ER

PL.: ERS

Exclamation or interjection to express hesitation. Remember this and you will not materially ERr.

ES

PL.: ESSES
("ESS" IS
ALSO OK)

Phonetic spelling of the letter "S." Remember this ESpecially.

ET

PL.: N/A

Colloquial variant (past tense) of "eat" and French- and Latin-origin term for "and." Remember this, ETcetera.

EW

PL.: N/A

Expression of disgust, pronounced "yeww." Fail to remember this and EW will be disgusted.

Note that the plural "ews" is not currently an official Scrabble word.

PL.: EXES

Former romantic partner, also the letter X (and, as a verb, to cross something out), and a Latin-derived term meaning "out of" or "from," as in "ex libris" or "ex cathedra." Remember this for a "deus EX machina" move.

F

FA

PL.: FAS

A note on the diatonic scale as used in the "solfège" or "sol-fa" method of syllabic musical notation and education ("do, re, mi, fa"). See "ut" for the origins of the system. Also popularized by Mad Magazine as an exclamation replacing the usual "ha" to denote laughter: "Fa fa fa!" Remember, so FA, so good.

FE

PL.: FES

A letter of the Hebrew alphabet. Remember that chemical symbols are not allowed in Scrabble, so the periodic symbol for iron, "FE," must be used only ironically.

FY

 CSW ONLY

PL.: N/A

An interjection indicating disgust or reproach, also "fye" and "fie." Remember to FYle this under FYne words.

G

GI

PL.: GIS

The jacket used in judo and other Japanese-origin martial arts, pronounced "gee," as in the exclamation of pleasant surprise. Remember this one for a pleasant surprise: "GI whiz!"

GO

PL.: GOS

To leave, depart, travel, move, or take a turn. Remember this when it's your GO.

GU

ⓘ **CSW ONLY**

PL.: GUS

Variant of "gju" (also CSW only): a type of stringed instrument from Shetland, used prior to the introduction of the fiddle. Remember not to get stuck in the GU.

H

HA
PL.: HAS

Exclamation of surprise or laughter. Remember this for a pleasant surprise that lets you use your awkward four-point "H" — "HA HA!"

HE
PL.: HES

Preferred pronoun of the masculine individual. Remember, HE who hesitates is toast.

HI
PL.: HIS

Interjection meaning "hello!" Remember this for a HI score.

HM
PL.: N/A

Expression of consternation, consideration or ongoing thought, to indicate the brain is working despite evidence to the contrary. "Hmm" is also an acceptable word. Remember this one when the tiles on the board make you go HMmmm...

HO
PL.: HOS

Another expression of surprise; "Ho! What's this?" Remember the gift of this oft-overlooked word as a present from Santa: "HO HO HO!"

I

ID
PL.: IDS

That impulsive and hedonistic part of the unconscious human psyche responsible for immediate pleasure-seeking or other emotion-sating behavior, moderated in the healthy individual by the ego and super-ego. Remember this, don't be an IDiot.

IF
PL.: IFS

Conditional conjunction expressing possibility. Remember what's possible IF you can keep your head when all about you are losing theirs.

IN
PL.: INS

Preposition used to include something within something else. Remember, the Devil is IN the detail.

IO
 CSW ONLY
PL.: IOS

An archaic triumphant exclamation, with the same pronunciation as the Chinese exclamation "ai-yo" which, however, expresses frustration or annoyance. IO it to myself to remember this.

IS
PL.: N/A

Third person singular present indicative of "to be." Remember, "this IS it."

IT

Third person singular neutral pronoun. To repeat, remember, "this is IT!"

PL.: ITS

J

JA

PL.: N/A

An affirmative reply or positive exclamation, pronounced "ya" and deriving from the German or Dutch, possibly via Afrikaans. Also the origin of "yeah." Remember, JA got to work with what JA got.

JO

PL.: N/A

Scottish term for "sweetheart" or "beau" (see also "BO") as used in the Robert Burns poem "John Anderson, My Jo." Remember this and be a regular JOe.

Note that the plural "jos" is not currently an official Scrabble word.

K

KA

PL.: KAS

A spiritual entity in Egyptian mythology, alongside the "ba" (see also) part of the human soul: the life force. Remember that the body is merely a vehicle for the spirit; a passenger KA, if you will.

KI

PL.: KIS

Variation of "qi" (see also), the human life energy or "force" in Chinese (and other Oriental) philosophy. Remember, every ka needs a KI.

KO

 CSW ONLY

PL.: KOS (CSW & NWL)

A Maori digging implement. Also a Japanese-origin term referring to a state that can arise in a game of the abstract strategy board game *Go*. The "ko rule" states that a move that replicates a player's immediately-previous position is forbidden. Remember this to K.O. your opponent.

KY

ⓘ **CSW ONLY**

PL.: N/A

Archaic Middle English plural term meaning "cows." Remember this to put the KYbosh on your opponent — or, alternatively, that the KY in KentuckY graze on blue grass.

LA
PL.: LAS

A note on the sol-fa diatonic scale (see "fa"). Remember this word and you'll be in LA LA LAnd.

LI
PL.: LIS

A traditional Chinese unit of distance measurement, sometimes (though rather inaccurately) known as the "Chinese mile." Historically-variable, but now set to one half-kilometer. Remember to be like Bruce LI, and let your words flow like water amongst the tiles.

LO
PL.: LOS (CSW ONLY)

Exclamation, often biblical, expressing surprise, astonishment, or to draw the listener's attention to a matter of importance or magnificence. Remember, a LO word can give a high score.

MA

PL.: MAS

Mother, in a surprising number of languages as well as English — presumably as it's the easiest and first sound a baby can reliably utter. Also "my" in many dialects. Remember to use your words like yer MA taught ya.

ME

PL.: MES

The first-person singular-case objective pronoun and for many the most important word in the English language. Remember, "ME first!"

MI

PL.: MIS

A note on the sol-fa diatonic scale (see "fa"). Remember do-re-MI, a name I call myself.

MM

PL.: N/A

Exclamation implying satisfaction or agreement. Remember to coMMit this to MMemory.

MO

PL.: MOS

Abbr. of "moment." Think for half a MO and you'll remember this one.

MU

PL.: MUS

A letter of the Greek alphabet, pronounced "moo" (US) or "mew" (UK). Remember, Greek cows say "MU" (Greek cats, if you're British).

PL.: N/A

The possessive case of the first-person singular, of great importance to the id-driven individual. Also an exclamation of surprise (contraction of "my word," "my goodness," etc.) Remember, "MY word! This is MY word."

N

NA

PL.: NAS (CSW ONLY)

A negative response: "no," "no way," etc. Remember, symbols of the periodic table are not allowed, so using sodium's would be iNAppropriate.

NE

PL.: N/A

Born with the name of ("né"), from the French. Masculine of the more common feminine "née" ("Mrs. Smith, née Jones"). Remember, French stallions say "NÉ."

NO

PL.: NOS, NOES

The primary negative adverb. Often the second word learned by babies, after "ma," and thereafter a lifelong favorite of the congenitally recalcitrant teenager and adult. Remember, often there is NO better word.

NU

PL.: NUS

A letter of the Greek alphabet, pronounced "noo" or "nyoo." Remember that a NU word can give NU opportunities.

NY

ⓘ CSW ONLY

PL.: NYS

Alternative spelling of "nigh" (near). Remember this when your hour of need draws NY — or, alternatively, "I Love N.Y."

OB

ⓘ **CSW ONLY**

PL.: OBS

An archaic term for "objection," also a similarly archaic term for the British half-penny, abbreviated from "obol" (a unit of ancient Greek currency, of low value). Early Greek obols were "spits" or rods/needles, usually of copper or bronze, which were in later eras developed into the more familiar and portable coin form.

Plutarch suggests that the Spartans' use of this iron rod "coinage" — impractical, bulky, and of negligible intrinsic value — was not evidence of backwardness but deliberately calculated to discourage avarice, greed, bribery, thievery, and building-up of stores of wealth, issuance of gold or silver coinage being expressly forbidden. "For who would steal, or receive as a bribe, or rob, or plunder that which could neither be concealed, nor possessed with satisfaction, nay, nor even cut to pieces with any profit?" (*Lycurgus*, chapter 9).

Remember, the OBol may be OBsolete, but do not OBject to using the word; quite the OBverse.

OD
PL.: ODS

A hypothetical force pronounced "odd" used by some (largely historical) practitioners to explain hypnosis and various quasi-spiritual phenomena, somewhat like the more modern "psi." Also "odyle" and other variations. Remember that an OD spelling can even-up your score.

OE
PL.: OES

An islet, pronounced "owe," from the Scandinavian, as in "Faroe" (possibly meaning "(the) island of sheep," etymology John Buchan evidently believed given his 1936 Richard Hannay novel of the same title). Also a Scottish exclamation (variant of "oy"). You OE it to yourself to remember this one.

OF
PL.: N/A

Preposition used to indicate possession, identity, reason, distance, etc. Remember to be OF good cheer.

OH
PL.: OHS

Exclamation of surprise or longing. If you fail to remember this you are likely to say "OH (expletive of choice)."

OI
PL.: OIS (CSW ONLY)

Uncouth British-origin term intended to attract the listener's (or prospective victim's) attention to the speaker, often as a precursor to the voicing of an objection, demand, complaint and/or as a precursor to ensuing physical altercation. Also a type of aggressive punk music prevalent in the 1970s and '80s UK scene. OI! You better remember this one — or else!

OK

PL.: OKAYS

Abbr. of "okay." A controversial recent addition to the word list but deemed acceptable in its lower-case form — as with other acronymously abbreviated phrases that have entered common lower-case usage, such as "radar" (RAdio Detection And Ranging) and even non-English-origin terms such as "flak" (German FLugzeugAbwehrKanone, literally "air-craft-defense cannon"). Remember, I'm OK, you're OK.

OM

PL.: OMS

Buddhist and Hindu sacred mystic syllable whose exact meaning and purpose varies depending upon religious tradition but generally referring to a divine energy. Do not OMit to remember this one.

ON

PL.: ONS

Physically supported by something, at a correct point ("on time," etc.) Remember this and you will be ON point.

Usage of the plural "ons" can mainly be found in references to the "on-side" in cricket, being the side of the field to which the batsman has his back: the bowler's right side, for a right-handed batsman; vice versa for a left-hander. The other side is the "off-side."

OO

ⓘ CSW ONLY

PL.: OOS

Scots word for "wool." Remember this word, don't be a fOOl: like James Bond, the double-O gives you a license to make a killer move.

OP

PL.: OPS

Abbr. of "optical," as in "op art" — a type of abstract visual art using optical illusions and similar effects. Also abbr. of "operation" (medical, military). Remember this for special OPs.

OR

PL.: ORS

Conjunction linking entities presented as alternatives, or providing alternate meanings. Remember to publish this word OR perish.

The plural "ors" is found mainly in reference to the alternate meaning of "Or" as the color gold in heraldry (deriving from the French for gold: "*or*," as in "*Palme d'Or*"). In this usage the word is often capitalized to distinguish it from the conjunction and prevent misunderstanding (otherwise one might reasonably ask "a Gryphon rampant or *what*?").

OS

PL.: OSSA, OSES

Latin-derived medical term for a bone; also a long ridge of gravel and sand (or "esker"). Remember this word to be bOSs.

OU

 CSW ONLY

PL.: OUS, OUENS

An informal South African term for a man ("bloke," "guy," etc.) deriving from the Dutch via Afrikaans. Remember, it's not what, it's OU — you know?

OW

PL.: N/A

Exclamation of pain. Remember to use your word pOWer.

OX

PL.: OXES,
OXEN

A domesticated bovine animal generally used for draught duties (cart-pulling, etc.) Usually though not exclusively a neutered male specimen (a "bull" being an intact male, generally unsuited for draught work due to his more excitable and boisterous temperament). Remember the animal's masculinity is thus less tOXic.

OY

PL.: OYS (CSW
ONLY)

Exclamation of frustration, pain or dismay, particularly when realizing one has failed to make an obvious play in a game of skill. Remember the word and you won't need to utter the exclamation, instead remarking "Oh, jOY!"

The plural "oys" refers to the word's alternate Scots meaning, "grandchild."

P

PA

PL.: PAS

Father, derived from the Latin "pater." Remember this word is PAr for the course.

The plural "pas" also refers to a dance move, as in "pas de deux."

PE

PL.: PES

A letter of the hebrew alphabet (and others), pronounced "pay" and origin of the Greek letter "pi" (see also) and the Latin "P." Remember to PE your dues.

The plural "pes" also refers to the foot-like part of certain creatures: the distal portion of tetrapodal animals' rear limbs.

PI

PL.: PIS

A letter of the Greek alphabet, origin of the Latin "P," and used in mathematics to represent the constant value of the ratio of a circle's circumference to its diameter. Remember this to get your slice of the PI.

PO

PL.: POS

Abbr. of "pot" as in "chamber pot" (rather archaic, chiefly British usage) — a portable toilet used historically in the bedroom prior to the advent of indoor plumbing, and still for medical purposes. Remember not to take one to a POt luck dinner.

Q

QI

PL.: QIS

The life force or universal power in Chinese and other Oriental philosophies (see also "ki," a variant spelling). Pronounced "chee." The plural "qis" is pronounced "cheese." Remember though that QI is not the singular of "cheese."

R

RE

PL.: RES

A note on the sol-fa diatonic scale, pronounced "ray" (see "fa"). Remember this word will be a RE of sunshine for your game.

The plural "res" also refers to a residence, or resolution (of a digital image).

S

SH
PL.: N/A

Interjection urging quiet or silence. Remember what wordSH SHean Connery would SHuggeSHt.

SI
PL.: SIS

A note on the sol-fa scale (see "fa") used as an alternative to the more common "ti" (see also), pronounced "see." SI why you should remember this?

The plural "sis" also refers to a sister.

SO
PL.: SOS

Consequently, in order that, in comparison, to such an extent. Remember, SO far, SO good.

ST
(i) **CSW ONLY**
PL.: N/A

Interjection expressing a wish for silence and attention; derived from "hist." Remember, STop STanding there and STart STicking it to your opponent!

T

TA

PL.: TAS

Britishism meaning "thank you." Originally baby-talk (according to the OED, at least) and now in common though informal use. Possibly related to one or more of the various Germanic languages' words for "thank you" such as "tak" (Danish), "Danke" (German), etc. Remember to say TA for the points!

TE

PL.: TES

Alternative spelling for the sol-fa (see "fa") note "ti" (see also), pronounced "tea." Also, in Taoism, the concept of human virtue or attainment in alignment with the tao (in this sense, it is pronounced "de," as in "coup de grace," and also alternately spelled "de"). Remember when it's time for TEa.

TI

PL.: TIS

A note on the sol-fa scale (See "fa"), also "te" (see also), pronounced "tea." Remember, I wouldn't forget this for all the TI in China.

TO

PL.: N/A

Infinitive marker, preposition indicating motion or in the direction of or alteration to something. Remembering this is TOo easy.

U

UG

CSW ONLY

PL.: UGS

An archaic Scottish and Northern English term for an emotion of fear, disgust, repulsion, etc. or an object of that emotion. Remember, it's an UGly feeling, but it could win you points.

UH

PL.: N/A

Expression of hesitation or uncertainty, sometimes also used as an affirmative (more commonly also with "-huh). Can you remember this? UH-huh, I think so.

UM

PL.: UMS

Another expression of hesitation or uncertainty. Remember, UM... Where was I?

UN

PL.: UNS

Contraction of "one" (as in "he's a good 'un"). Remember, this is UNforgettable.

UP

PL.: UPS

From a lower point to a higher one, a raising direction, an increase. Remember to use this before your time's UP.

UR

CSW ONLY

PL.: N/A

Interjection expressing hesitation or... What's that word for when one can't remember a word? Oh right, lethologica. Remember this — it's URgent!

US

PL.: N/A

First person plural objective case pronoun, also (informally) "me." Remember, you can't ask "Give US a clue?"

UT

PL.: UTS

Another musical note, for once not from the current sol-fa system but from the precursor thereof, introduced in the eleventh century by one Guido d'Arrezo, a melodic monk considered the father of musical notation. This original system derives its syllables from the hymn "Ut queant laxis" (also known as "Hymnus in Ioannem," being dedicated to Saint John the Baptist), the first stanza of which is: "UT queant laxis / REsonare fibris / MIra gestorum / FAmuli tuorum / SOLve polluti / LAbii reatum / Sancte Iohannes." The first syllable of each line (with the exception of the last, where the saint's initials are used) gives us "ut, re, mi, fa, sol, la, si." The initial "ut" note was later replaced (with the "open syllable" "do"), presumably due to the original's guttural and "closed" nature making it rather difficult to sing. Remember this to pUT your opponent in his/her place.

V

There are no "V" two-letter words.
Frustrating, isn't it?

W

WE

PL.: N/A

First person plural nominative case pronoun. The "royal we," also known as the "majestic plural" ("pluralis maiestatis" in the Latin) refers to the bizarre but common habit of monarchs to discuss themselves in the plural, whereas the tendency in other less exalted individuals is known as "nosism" (from the Latin "nos" — "we"). Remember, WE are not amused.

WO

PL.: WOS, WOES

Variant of "woe" or, depending on who you believe, "whoa." Remember to ask, as did Sophocles, "What WO is lacking, to my tale of WOes?"

X

XI

PL.: XIS

The fourteenth letter of the Greek alphabet, pronounced "sigh," origin of our letter "X" and in astronomy the fourteenth star in a given constellation. Plural "xis." Remember, XIs matters.

XU

PL.: N/A

Vietnamese monetary unit, equal to one hundredth of a dong. Pronounced "sou," like the French word from which it derives, a "sou" being a five-centime coin and, more generally, referring to any small or negligible amount of money as in "I haven't a sou." Remember, so XU me!

Y

YA

PL.: YAS

Variant of "yes," also "you" or "your." Remember, YA got to work with what YA got.

The plural "yas" refers to another alternate definition of "ya" — a type of pear from the Far East, also known as the Chinese White pear.

YE

PL.: YES

Archaic plural of "thou." Also an archaic spelling of "the" with the "y" representing "th" — so "ye olde" is pronounced "the old," not "yee oldee" ("olde" is itself an artificial archaism, having been created in the nineteenth century to add an air of aged venerability to commercial endeavors). Remember, "YE gods!"

The plural "yes" is, of course, the affirmative reply.

YO

PL.: N/A

Informal American greeting. Remember this one, don't be a YOYO.

YU

CSW ONLY

PL.: YUS

Archaic term for a type of jade, deriving from the Chinese for jade, "yu" (as in "yu chu" — "jade jewel.") Remember this — YU won't be sorry.

Z

ZA

PL.: ZAS

Abbr. of "pizza" and one of the few examples of a word being abbreviated head-first, probably because the alternative abbreviation "pi" would sound rather unappetizing. Remembering this one will ZAp your opponent.

ZE

 CSW ONLY

PL.: N/A

A gender-neutral pronoun and recent addition. Remember this and you'll be good from A to ZEe (ZEd, if you're British).

ZO

CSW ONLY

PL.: ZOS

A breed of Tibetan cattle, also spelled "dzo," "zho," "dzho," and "dso," all of which variants are found in CSW but none in NWL. The zo is in fact a hybrid between yak and domestic cow, for which other words have also been suggested: "yakow," which is found in CSW, though not NWL, and "yattle," which is found in neither, presumably due to its absurdity. Remember the motto of the Tibetan cowboy: "ZO far, ZO good!"

NWL ALPHABETICAL LIST

- AA AB AD AE AG AH AI AL AM AN AR AS AT AW AX AY
- BA BE BI BO BY
- DA DE DO
- ED EF EH EL EM EN ER ES ET EW EX
- FA FE
- GI GO
- HA HE HI HM HO
- ID IF IN IS IT
- JO
- KA KI
- LA LI LO
- MA ME MI MM MO MU MY
- NA NE NO NU
- OD OE OF OH OI OK OM ON OP OR OS OW OX OY

- PA PE PI PO
- QI
- RE
- SH SI SO
- TA TE TI TO
- UH UM UN UP US UT
- WE WO
- XI XU
- YA YE YO
- ZA

NWL ALPHABETICAL LIST BY LAST LETTER

- AA BA DA FA HA KA LA MA NA PA TA YA ZA
- AB
- AD ED ID OD
- AE BE DE FE HE ME NE OE PE RE TE WE YE
- EF IF OF
- AG
- AH EH OH SH UH
- AI BI GI HI KI LI MI OI PI QI SI TI XI
- OK
- AL EL
- AM EM HM MM OM UM
- AN EN IN ON UN

- BO DO GO HO JO LO MO NO PO SO TO WO YO
- OP UP
- AR ER OR
- AS ES IS OS US
- AT ET IT UT
- MU NU XU
- AW EW OW
- AX EX OX
- AY BY MY OY

CSW ALPHABETICAL LIST

- AA AB AD AE AG AH AI AL AM AN AR AS AT AW AX AY
- BA BE BI BO BY
- CH
- DA DE DI DO
- EA ED EE EF EH EL EM EN ER ES ET EW EX
- FA FE FY
- GI GO GU
- HA HE HI HM HO
- ID IF IN IO IS IT
- JA JO
- KA KI KO KY
- LA LI LO
- MA ME MI MM MO MU MY
- NA NE NO NU NY

- OB OD OE OF OH OI OK OM ON OO OP OR OS OU OW OX OY
- PA PE PI PO
- QI
- RE
- SH SI SO ST
- TA TE TI TO
- UG UH UM UN UP UR US UT
- WE WO
- XI XU
- YA YE YO YU
- ZA ZE ZO

CSW ALPHABETICAL LIST BY LAST LETTER

- AA BA DA EA FA HA JA KA LA MA NA PA TA YA ZA
- AB OB
- AD ED ID OD
- AE BE DE EE FE HE ME NE OE PE RE TE WE YE ZE
- EF IF OF
- AG UG
- AH CH EH OH SH UH
- AI BI DI GI HI KI LI MI OI PI QI SI TI XI
- OK
- AL EL
- AM EM HM MM OM UM
- AN EN IN ON UN

- BO DO GO HO IO JO KO LO MO NO OO PO SO TO WO YO ZO
- OP UP
- AR ER OR UR
- AS ES IS OS US
- AT ET IT ST UT
- GU MU NU OU XU YU
- AW EW OW
- AX EX OX
- AY BY FY KY MY NY OY

NOTES

Made in United States
North Haven, CT
12 October 2023

42643471R10049